CW00841297

# AWESOME
# RIDDLES
## FOR SMART KIDS

### 365+ TRICKY QUESTIONS
### AND BRAIN TEASERS

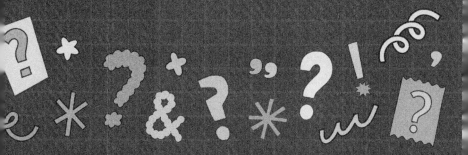

Produced by Beaky and Starlight Ltd.

Published: June 2023

ISBN: 9798398937459

For more information about the publisher, please visit:

www.facebook.com/BeakyAndStarlight/

# CONTENTS

----------------------------

# INTRODUCTION

---------------------------------------

Welcome to the world of riddles! I'm so excited to have you here. These riddles are sure to test your brainpower and your wit. Some of them are easy, but some of them will really make you think. I hope you enjoy the challenge!

Here are a few tips for solving riddles:

**Tip #1: Think outside the box.** Riddles often require creative thinking and looking at things from different angles. Don't be afraid to explore possibilities and come up with unexpected answers.

**Tip #2: Pay attention to the details!** Riddles often involve wordplay, puns, and clever tricks. Take your time to understand every word and sentence in the riddle. Sometimes, the tiniest clue can hold the key to unravelling the riddle's secret.

**Tip #3: Practice, practice, practice.** The more riddles you solve, the better you become at deciphering them. So, don't give up! Keep practising and challenging yourself with new riddles.

**Tip #4: Have fun!** Riddles are all about having a great time. Share them with your friends and family, and who knows, you might uncover a fresh perspective or even stumble upon a hilariously silly answer!

Get ready to unleash your super-duper problem-solving powers as we dive into the wacky realm of riddles!

# RIDDLES

1. What is so fragile that saying its name breaks it?

2. What two things you can never eat for breakfast?

3. What has a neck but no head?

4. What has 6 faces and 21 eyes, but can't smile?

WHAT AM I?

5. Mr and Mrs Smith have 6 daughters and each daughter has 1 brother. How many people are in the Smith family?

6. I'm white when I'm dirty but black when I'm clean. What am I?

7. Lucy's father has 3 children called Snap, Crackle, and... ?

8. What is brown, has a tail, a head, but no legs?

9. Two dads and two sons went fishing on the lake. They caught three fish which was enough for them each to take home one fish. How was this possible?

10. What English word is pronounced the same if you take away 4 of its 5 letters?

11. What message does this picture say?

12. If 10 plus 3 equals 1, then what does 8 plus 6 equal?

13. Without using plus, minus, times or divide how can you make the number 7 even?

14. Josh ordered a new fishing rod online to be delivered to his house on a little island. The fishing rod was 212 cm long, however, the island postal service only carried items up to 210cm long. How did Josh still manage to receive the rod without it being broken or dismantled in any way?

15. Name 3 days of the week without using the words Monday, Tuesday, Wednesday, Thursday, Friday, Saturday, or Sunday.

16. You leave more behind the more you take. What am I?

17. What goes up when the rain comes down?

18. I'm full of holes but still good at holding water. What am I?

19. I get bigger the more you take away. What am I?

20. A girl was visiting a village fete and went to a stall where a man said, "If I write your exact weight on a piece of paper then you give me £5, but if I can't do that then I'll give you £5". The girl couldn't see any scales nearby so thought it was worth a go, but she ended up having to pay the man £5. How did he get the correct answer?

21. Some months have 31 days, some have 30 days but how many months have 28 days?

22. If you share me then you lose me, but if you have me then you want to share me. What am I?

23. What has a head, 4 legs, but just 1 foot?

24. Jon was running a cross-country race and passed the person in 2nd place just before the finish. What position did Jon finish in the race?

25. What belongs to you, but other people use it more than you do?

26. A clever teacher was in a small town on holiday and needed to get a haircut. This town had 2 hairdressing shops next to each other. The teacher looked in the first shop and saw a hairdresser looking untidy with badly cut hair and in need of a shave. He looked in the second shop and saw a freshly shaved barber with a very well-styled neat haircut. Which shop did the teacher go to for a haircut and why?

27. I don't breathe but I do need air, if you feed me then I'll grow, but if you give me water I'll die. What am I?

28. What happens twice in a millisecond, once in a minute, but never in a year?

29. What gets wetter the more it dries?

30. What's the picture trying to tell us?

31. You don't wear me but I cover your body. The more you use me the thinner I get. What am I?

32. What can't you put into a saucepan?

33. What two-word phrase does this picture say?

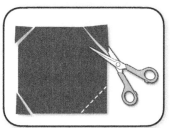

34. When Abi was 8 her sister was half her age. Abi is now 10, so how old is her sister?

35. What 3 numbers, bigger than 0, give the same total when added together as when they are multiplied together?

36. Which is heavier: a kilogram of potatoes or a kilogram of feathers?

37. What goes all around the world but never leaves the corner?

38. What has keys but no locks, you can enter and there is space but you can't go inside?

39. What can you hold in your right hand but not in your left hand?

40. You will find me in Earth, Mercury, Mars, and Jupiter but not in Neptune or Venus. What am I?

41. I'm orange and sound like a parrot. What am I?

42. Which 5-letter word becomes shorter when you add 2 letters to it?

43. What needs to be broken to use it?

44. I'm tall when I'm young, but short when I'm old. What am I?

45. I can fill a room but not take up any space. What am I?

46. Where does Thursday come before Wednesday?

47. Can a kangaroo jump higher than a building?

48. What's the message this image trying to say?

NE **FRIEND** ED = DE **FRIEND** ED

49. During which month do people sleep the least?

50. I'm here today but tomorrow there will be more of me. As the weeks pass by I will drift away, but will be replaced with more of me. I'm what you've seen but not what you see. What am I?

51. Steve, Simon, Sarah, and Susanne were in an empty square room. There wasn't any furniture or any shelves. Where could Sarah place an apple such that everyone apart from Steve could see it?

52. How can you get 4 by taking away 2 from 5?

53. What two-word phrase does the picture suggest?

54. There are 2 ducks in front of a duck, and 2 ducks behind a duck. In the middle is a duck. How many ducks are there in total?

55. If 4 cats take 4 minutes to catch 4 mice, how long does it take for 1 cat to catch a mouse?

56. How many times can you subtract 6 from 36?

57. A wheel has 32 spokes, how many spaces are there between the spokes?

58. Where do you find forests without trees and roads without cars?

59. I go up and down at the same time, I am present tense and past tense too. What am I?

60. My first 2 letters are male, my first 3 letters female, my first 4 letters mean someone brave and courageous, and altogether I'm a great woman. What am I?

61. Dylan was feeling generous and wanted to pay for his friends to go to the movies with him. Would it be cheaper for him to take 2 friends with him at the same time, or to take 1 friend to 2 different films?

62. What two-word phrase does the picture on the right suggest?

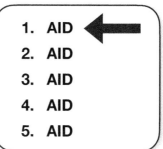

1. AID
2. AID
3. AID
4. AID
5. AID

63. What starts with E, ends with E but only has one letter in it?

64. I am the weirdest creature you'll ever find. I have two eyes in front and many more behind. What am I?

65. I am a bird, I am a fruit, and I'm also a person. What am I?

66. It was a warm sunny day, and next to the river were two foxes that needed to get to the other side. It was too deep to walk across, too wide to swim across, but luckily there was a small boat able to take one fox at a time. The boat needed a fox in it to steer it across but will sink if two foxes were both on it. They crossed the river successfully. How?

67. What message does
    the picture on the
    right say?

> **Arrest**
> ———————
> **You're**

68. What can be white, dirty, bold-faced, big, and wicked?

69. What can you break even if you don't touch it, or drop it?

70. If I bought a racing bike for £800 then sold it for £1000, then bought it back again a month later for £1100 and sold it again for £1300 – how much money would I have made?

71. What two keys can't open any doors?

72. Which invention lets you see through a wall?

73. I build a home in the air,

   with silk so fine and fair.

   I'm small, but I'm not weak,

   I'm a creature you might fear. What am I?

74. What name does this picture say?

75. What goes down and up but never moves?

76. What has legs but doesn't walk?

77. What can't you throw but you can catch?

78. What runs around a garden yet never moves?

79. What smells better than it tastes?

80. If 2 is a company, and 3 is a crowd, then what are 4 and 5?

81. The day before yesterday I was 11 and next year I'll be 14. When is my birthday?

82. Alice has as many brothers as sisters, but each brother has only half as many brothers as sisters. How many sisters and brothers are there in Alice's family?

83. Forward I'm heavy but backwards I'm not. What am I?

84. Which word of five letters has one left when two are removed?

85. The person who makes it doesn't want it, the person who buys it doesn't use it, and the person who uses it doesn't see it. What is it?

86. The rich man wants it, the poor man has it, you bring it with you when you die, it's more evil than the devil and greater than God. What is it?

87. First, think of the colour of the clouds.

    Next, think of the colour of the snow.

    Now, think of the colour of a bright full moon.

    Now answer quickly what do cows drink?

88. What does an elephant have but no other animal has, that prevents them from going extinct?

89. What two-word phrase is this picture trying to say?

90. I'm at the beginning of the end, and the end of space and time. I surround every place and essential to creation. What am I?

91. I live in a little house on my own, it has no windows and no doors. To get out I need to break through the wall. What am I?

92. What is black when you buy it, red when you use it, and grey when you throw it away?

93. I run in and out of the town all day and night. What am I?

94. Which English word has 3 sets of double letters consecutively?

95. I'm green, then brown, and when the wind blows I fall down. What am I?

96. I don't bend, sometimes I am your enemy sometimes your friend. What am I?

97. Can you work out how to make the total 100 using four 9s?

98. What is seen in the middle of March and April but not at the start or end of either month?

99. Your mother's brother's only brother-in-law has just knocked on your front door. Who is it?

100. What does this picture say?

FUNNY FUNNY

WORDS WORDS WORDS WORDS

101. If you take 2 apples from a bowl of 3 apples, how many would you have?

102. How much dirt is in a hole that is 1 metre deep by 50cm wide?

103. Where is the only place in the world where today comes before yesterday?

104. Which word in the dictionary is spelled incorrectly?

105. John is is six feet tall, he works at a butcher's, and he wears size eleven shoes. What does he weigh?

106. What five-letter word written in all capital letters can be read the same upside down?

107. What starts with a P, ends with an E and contains a lot of letters?

108. What starts at zero, goes up and up, but never comes down?

109. What should you always keep after giving it to someone?

110. What is a safe way to drop a raw egg from a height onto a concrete floor so it doesn't break?

YOU SURE I'LL BE ALRIGHT IN THIS?

# RIDDLES

111. What starts with T, ends with T, and contains T within it?

112. I have a long tongue but I'm not an anteater,

    I have a long neck but I'm not a swan,

    I eat leaves but I'm not a koala,

    I have spots but I'm not a leopard.

    What am I?

113. What is the longest word in the dictionary?

114. You can pick me up with ease, but throwing me is not easy, no matter how strong you are. What am I?

115. Cut me open and tears won't roll down my cheeks, but they might roll down yours. What am I?

116. I am everywhere, yet can't be seen,

    I pass through forests, making trees lean.

    I run through the sea, making waves high,

    Catch me if you can, give it a try.

    What am I?

117. What question can you never truthfully answer yes to?

118. What message is this picture trying to say?

119. What is something that you bury when it's alive and dig up when it's dead?

120. Harry points at a picture and says, "I don't have any brothers or sisters, but this man's dad is my dad's son." Who is in the picture?

121. What kind of tree can you carry in your hand?

122. How do you make the number one disappear?

123. What does this picture say?

124. Without a mouth, I can still speak, unseen by any eye, yet heard nonetheless, what am I?

125. I can be cracked, made, told, and played. What am I?

126. I am always in front of you, but can't be seen. What am I?

127. Which cheese is made backwards?

128. What has a bottom at the top?

129. The more there is, the less you see. What am I?

130. You will always find two of me,

    Identical in shape and anatomy.

    We both can hear and both can feel,

    But meeting each other is never real.

    What are we?

131. I'm a creature with three eyes, lined up in a row. If my red eye opens, you must stop and not go. What am I?

132. On top of a barn, a rooster perches with great poise. If it laid an egg, in which direction would the egg roll down?

133. What has a face and two hands but no arms or legs?

134. If you're not careful, I'll easily break, but smile at me and I'll smile back. What am I?

135. A pencil case and a ruler together cost $12. The pencil case costs $10 more than the ruler. How much does the ruler cost?

136. Your dad went to the store to buy a dozen eggs, but unfortunately on the way home all but eight of them broke. Can you guess how many eggs are left unbroken?

137. It's the middle of the night and snowflakes are falling, but the weather forecast says that tomorrow and the following day will be clear. Can you predict if the sun will be shining 48 hours from now?

138. What goes down to make us stay, or comes up to let us go?

139. In a farm, there is one farmer, 2 dogs, 3 pigs, 10 cows, and 25 sheep. How many feet are there in the farm?

140. What does this picture say?

141. I am at home on a tree but never go inside. If I fall off, I will surely die. What am I?

142. I show up in winter, but I perish in summer. I grow towards the ground. What am I?

143. I can go through glass without breaking it. What am I?

144. What gets sharper the more you use it?

145. I'm a ball that rolls but can't be bounced,

    Inside your head is where I'm housed.

    I come in many different shades.

    What am I?

146. What word does this picture say?

147. What do you call a bear without teeth?

148. What has four fingers and a thumb, is warm but not alive?

149. Tomorrow is not Wednesday or Thursday.

    Yesterday was not Friday or Saturday.

    Today is not Thursday or Monday.

    What day is today?

150. I'm a green house. Inside my green house, there is a white house. Inside my white house, there is a red house. Inside my red house, there are lots of babies. What am I?

151. How far can a fox run into the woods?

152. What has 88 keys, but cannot open a single door?

153. Two in a corner. One in a room. Zero in a house. But one in a shelter. What am I?

154. Three doctors call Andy their brother, but Andy denied having any brothers. How many brothers does Andy actually have?

155. What falls a lot but doesn't get hurt at all?

156. I'm in the month of December, but not in any other month. I am not a holiday. What am I?

157. Which vehicle can be written identically both forwards and backwards?

158. If the day before yesterday is the 3rd, then what is the day after tomorrow?

159. Mary and Lisa were born to the same mother, on the same day, in the same month, and in the same year, but they're not twins. How is this possible?

160. William, Allison, and Elliot are drinking coffee. Emily, Michael, and Rachel are drinking tea. Following this pattern, is Tilly drinking coffee or tea?

161. What can be cut on a table but is never eaten?

162. What does this picture say?

ABCDEFGHI

JKLMNOPQR

ST  VWXYZ

163. What invention lets you walk right through a wall?

164. Jack is in a dark room with a candle, a wood stove, and an oil lamp. He only has one match. What should he light first?

165. Pete is younger than Dan but older than Ben. Annie is older than Becky and younger than Dan. Becky is older than Pete. Who is the middle child?

166. You can see me in water, but I never get wet. What am I?

167. Lily loves pink. She lives in a one-storey house in which everything is pink. Pink walls, pink doors, pink furniture. Can you guess what colour are the stairs?

168. A girl fell off a 20-foot ladder. She wasn't hurt. Why?

169. What does this picture say?

170. A bus driver was heading down a busy street. He went past a few stop signs without stopping, went the wrong way on a one-way street, and used his phone. But he didn't break any traffic laws. How?

171. My thunder comes before the lightning. My lightning comes before the clouds. My rain dries all the land it touches. What am I?

172. Once upon a time, there was a farmer who needed to cross a river. He had a bag of corn, a hen, and a fox, but his boat could only carry one thing with him at a time. However, there was a problem: if the hen was left alone with the corn, she would gobble it all up. And if the hen was left alone with the fox, the fox would make a meal out of her. How can the farmer safely take all three things across the river without any harm?

173. A man dies of old age on his 25th birthday. How is this possible?

174. The man calls his dog from the opposite side of the river, and the dog manages to cross the river without getting wet or using a bridge or boat. How is this possible?

175. What comes once in a minute, twice in a moment, but never in a thousand years?

176. How is seven different from the rest of the numbers between one and 10?

177. A group of seven people meet for the first time. They each shake hands with everyone else once. What is the total number of handshakes?

178. Stuck in an eerie house where the power is cut off, your only way out is through one of three rooms. The first room contains a very hungry lion, the second room is filled with thick smoke and poisonous snakes, and the third room is flooded with ankle-depth water and has some exposed electrical wires. Which room will you choose to escape?

179. What word is this picture trying to say?

180. I sometimes run, but I cannot walk. You always follow me around. What am I?

181. Where does one wall meet the other wall?

182. A tiny bead, like fragile glass, strung along a cord of grass. What is it?

183. Bob, Sarah and Alice cycled to school. Between them, they have 3 bike wheels. How is this possible?

184. Anna's mother has three kids. The first one is called May and the second one is June. Can you guess the third one's name?

185. What is the end of everything?

186. Born in an instant, I tell all stories. I can be lost, but I never die. What am I?

187. Which phrase does this picture say?

188. While driving his black truck with no light on and no moon in sight, a man spotted a lady in a dark dress crossing the street. How was he able to see her?

189. What shape has no angles but is not a circle?

190. What is the worst vegetable to have on a boat?

191. What kind of room has no doors or windows?

192. What has words, but never speaks?

193. Jerry made an order for pizza. All of them are Margherita except one, and all of them are Hawaiian except one. How many did he order?

194. What fruit is always sad?

195. One rabbit saw a group of 9 elephants while going to the river. Every elephant saw 3 monkeys going toward the river. Each monkey had a parrot in each hand. How many animals were going towards the river?

196. My pocket is empty, yet I have one thing in it. What is it?

197. Turn me on my side, and I am without bounds. Cut me in half and I am nothing. What am I?

198. A maths book complains to a history book. What does it say?

199. A train leaves from London towards Edinburgh at a speed of 100 mph. Half an hour later, a train leaves from Edinburgh towards London at 120 mph. Assuming there is a distance of exactly 335 miles between London and Edinburgh, which train is closer to London when they meet?

200. What book won't teachers give you credit for reading?

201. They arrive in the night without being summoned. In the day, they vanish without being taken. They take nothing but hold answers to many things. What are they?

202. Peel away the skin, cook it with pride,

Savour the taste as you take a bite.

Discard the core, no need to keep,

Tell me, what did you just eat?

203. I know a word of letters three. Add two and fewer there will be. What is the word?

204. What room do ghosts avoid?

205. There is an empty fruit bowl, 25 cm in diameter and 20 cm deep. How many oranges can you put in this empty fruit bowl?

206. Which two-word phrase does this picture say?

207. I have no eyes, legs, or ears but I help move the earth. What am I?

208. Dan drives a car to work. The car has six wheels. How is it possible?

209. What are moving left to right at this very minute?

210. I am essential for life,

but I can also be destructive.

I can be found in three different forms,

and I am always in you.

What am I?

211. What can you taste every
day but should never eat?

I'M BACK!

212. Alice throws a ball as far as
she can and it comes back to
her straight away without anyone
or anything touching it. How is
it possible?

213. People want to make me. Some save me.
Others change me. And some raise me.
What am I?

214. What single digit appears most frequently
between and including the numbers 1
and 100?

215. What four-letter word can be written forwards, backwards, or upside down, and still be read from left to right?

216. I know a word that contains six letters. If you remove one letter, 12 remain. What is it?

217. What cannot be seen, has no weight, but when added to a barrel, it reduces the barrel's overall weight?

218. I build up castles.

    I tear down mountains.

    I make some men blind,

    I help others to see.

    What am I?

219. What place is this picture trying to say?

220. Emma ordered a fast-delivery pizza. It arrived the next year and she was happy. How?

221. A man built a house with all sides facing south. While looking out the window one day, he spotted a large bear walking by. What colour was the bear?

222. How many 9s are there between 1 and 100?

223. What should you place between 3 and 4 to make it bigger than 3 but smaller than 4?

224. What is black and white and blue?

225. What does this picture say?

MCE
MCE
MCE

226. When asked about his age, John replied, "In two years I will be twice as old as I was five years ago." How old is John?

227. What word in English has three syllables and 26 letters?

228. Two hours ago, it was as long after one o'clock in the afternoon as it was before one o'clock in the morning. What time is it now?

229. What is the thing that you can hold without touching and is harder to catch the faster you run?

230. You buy me taken apart,

    To redo what has been undone;

    Four of my pieces have one sharp corner,

    The rest of them have none.

    What am I?

231. It's red, blue, purple and green, no one can reach it, not even the queen. What is it?

232. What has an eye but cannot see?

233. I have a skin and many eyes. When cooked, I'm a tasty surprise. What am I?

234. I am bought but not kept. I am large and small. I can be any shape. What am I?

235. Three little letters, a paradox to some. The worse that it is, the better it becomes. What is it?

236. The zookeeper rewarded the animals with money. The ostrich got $10, the butterfly got $30, and the spider got $40. What did the lion receive?

237. What colour is the wind?

238. What is higher without the head than with it?

239. What does this picture say?

240. People buy me to eat, but never eat me. What am I?

241. What kind of ship has two mates but no captain?

242. What becomes smaller when you turn it upside down?

243. There is a pit that is 20 metres deep. At the bottom of the pit there is a snail. Every day, the snail manages to climb up 5 metres. However, during the night, it slides back down 4 metres. How many days will it take for the snail to escape the hole?

244. What word does this picture say?

245. If you multiply this number by any other number, the answer will always be the same. What number is this?

246. I have a leg but I do not move, a face but no expression, be it wind or rain I stay outside. What am I?

247. I sound like one letter, but I'm written with three. I show you things, when you look through me. What am I?

248. You're driving a bus. At the first stop, 10 passengers boarded the bus. At the second stop, 1 passenger got off while 5 others hopped on. At the third stop, 3 people got off and 2 got on. Finally, at the fourth stop, 5 passengers got off and 7 got on. What's the name of the bus driver?

249. What walks on four legs in the morning, two legs in the afternoon, three legs in the evening, and no legs at night?

250. What question can be asked repeatedly throughout the day, and the answer will always be different, but still correct?

251. Which letter of the alphabet has the most water?

252. You see a boat filled with people, yet there is not a single person on board. How is that possible?

253. What breaks yet never falls, and what falls yet never breaks?

254. If everyone bought a white car, what would we have?

255. If today is Monday, what is the day after the day before the day before tomorrow?

256. Until I am measured I am not known,
Yet how you miss me when I have flown.

257. In the morning, I'm by your feet,

All day long, I won't retreat.

Under the midday sun, I'm nearly gone,

But morning and evening, I linger on.

What am I?

258. Three men were in a boat when it capsized, but only two got their hair wet. Why?

259. How is it physically possible for you to stand behind your father and for your father to stand behind you at the same time?

260. What happens when you throw a red rock into a yellow stream?

261. I fly without wings, I cry without eyes. What am I?

262. What 8-letter word can have consecutive letters taken out and still remain a word until only one letter is left?

263. What does this picture say?

264. When my dad was 31, I was just 8 years old. Now his age is twice as old as my age. What is my current age?

265. They are many and one, they wave and they drum. You take them with you everywhere. What are they?

266. What can make an octopus laugh?

267. If it takes 6 men 6 days to dig 6 holes, how long will it take one man to dig half a hole?

268. A is the father of B. B is the brother of C. C is the father of D. How is D related to A?

269. I am a seed with three letters in my name. Take away two and I still sound the same. What am I?

270. What does this picture say?

> **A B C D E F G H**
>
> **J M O P Q R S T**
>
> **U V W X Y Z**

271. There are five sisters in the lounge and they are all busy. Ann is reading a book, Bella is drawing, Carol is playing chess, and Diane is listening to music. What is the 5th sister doing?

272. What clothing does a house wear?

273. What asks no questions but requires many answers?

274. What was the highest mountain in the world before Mount Everest was discovered?

275. A 300-foot train travelling at 300 feet per minute enters a 300-foot tunnel. How long does it take the train to pass through the tunnel?

276. I am a word that belongs in a gallery, but if you add a single letter, I become a word associated with a racetrack. What word am I?

277. We are brothers who bear burdens all day, yet we are full while active and empty at rest. What are we?

278. What is one thing that the letter "T" and an island have in common?

279. He has one.

A person has two.

A citizen has three.

A human being has four.

A personality has five.

An inhabitant of the earth has seven.

What am I?

280. A person lives on the 15th floor of a building. When he goes out, he takes the elevator to the ground floor. But when he comes back, he takes the elevator only to the 8th floor and then uses the stairs to reach the apartment on the 15th floor. The only time he takes the elevator to the 15th floor is on rainy days. Why?

281. How many sides does a circle have?

282. What does this picture say?

283. Alice had some cookies. After eating one, she divided the remaining cookies in half with her sister, ate another, and then shared half of what was left with her brother. Alice ended up with 4 cookies. How many did Alice originally have?

284. What do you call a magician who lost his magic?

285. If a monkey, a bird, and a squirrel race up a coconut tree, who do you think will grab the banana first?

286. What is it that when you remove the whole, you still have some left over?

287. What sounds like a sneeze and is made out of leather?

288. Which letter in the alphabet is always asking questions?

289. What can never be burned in a fire nor drowned in water?

290. A man sat in a dark house at night with no light sources. Surprisingly, he was contently reading a book. How?

291. What do you get if you put a radio in the fridge?

292. How is it possible for a horse to reach its food when it is 20 metres away and the rope tied to it is only 19 metres long?

293. What has teeth but doesn't bite?

I WON'T BITE I PROMISE!

294. What breaks in the water but never on land?

295. There are 4 black socks, 6 blue socks, 4 yellow socks, and 8 brown socks in a drawer. You are in the dark and can't see the socks. How many socks do you need to pull out to make sure you have a matching pair?

296. What does this picture say?

297. You have three boxes. One says "Apples," another says "Oranges," and the last one says "Apples and Oranges." You know that all the labels are incorrect, but you can only take out one fruit from one box. How can you figure out the correct labels for all the boxes?

298. Seven kids tried to fit under a small umbrella, none of them got wet. How did they do it?

299. What's always found on the ground but never gets dirty?

300. The cowboy rides in town on Friday, stays for three days, and then leaves on Friday. How?

301. I can travel from there to here by disappearing, and here to there by reappearing. What am I?

302. I am big on Saturday and Sunday. Small on Tuesday, Wednesday, and Thursday. I'm not on Monday or Friday. What am I?

303. What does this picture say?

304. I go through a door, yet never enter or exit. What am I?

305. What can be filled with empty hands?

306. What's the centre of gravity?

307. Paul and Jane are far away from each other, but Paul wants to send Jane a surprise gift. They want to make sure the gift is safe during shipping so decide to use locks to protect it. They each have their own lock but do not have access to the other person's key. What should they do to make sure the package is locked at all times during shipping yet Jane will be able to open the present?

308. There was a tree that grew twice as tall every year until it reached its full height after ten years. How many years did it take to reach half of its maximum height?

309. I provide food before I'm alive, while I'm alive, and after I'm dead. What am I?

310. A square has two, a line has one, and a point has zero. What is it?

311. A rectangle has three, a circle has two, and a square has one. What is it?

312. If 24 H in a D means "24 hours in a day", what do the following abbreviations mean:

    a) 60 S in a M
    e) 5 F on a H

    b) 28 D in F
    f) 2 E on Y F

    c) 12 M in a Y
    g) 7 H P B

    d) 4 S in a Y
    h) 8 P of the M

313. What can you sit on, sleep on, and brush your teeth with?

314. Jon managed to go for 23 days without sleep. How did he do it?

315. What fruit has its seeds on the outside?

316. A woman got a phone call from the police. They told her something very sad - her husband had been killed! They asked her to come to the crime scene right away. She quickly drove there, which took her about 20 minutes. But when she arrived, the police arrested her for the crime. How did they know she did it?

317. You may have heard the saying about there being a pot of gold at the end of a rainbow, but what really is at the end of a rainbow?

318. What does this picture say?

**Y Y Y MEN**

319. What is born long, dies short, and spends its life leaving a trail?

320. How many days are there in a span of four years?

321. Two people were born at exactly the same moment. However, they don't have the same birthdays. How is this possible?

322. In the cold of winter, I am formed. Despite having eyes, I cannot see, and though I have a nose, I cannot smell. What am I?

323. I can be written, I can be spoken, I can be exposed, I can be broken. What am I?

324. I suck and make a really loud sound. I am named after nothing and I move around. What am I?

325. What does this picture say?

326. Why are people so tired in April?

327. Despite my limited vision, I'm able to navigate my surroundings. While I do have legs, I mostly use them for sleeping. What am I?

328. When I was young, I had a tail and no legs. As I grew older, I lost my tail and acquired legs. What am I?

329. What has four wheels and flies?

330. What can you blow up and yet still keep unharmed?

331. A brick weighs 1 kilogram plus half of its weight. What is the total weight of the brick?

332. Abbie cut a 12-inch rope into equal sections. She made 3 cuts. What is the length of each section of the rope now?

333. Kevin was sitting on a park bench when a rich man joined him. Kevin boasted to the rich man that he knew almost every song that ever existed.

The rich man laughed and said, "I don't believe you! Sing a song with my daughter's name, Lily Johnson, in it, and I'll give you all the money in my wallet."

Kevin sang a song and won the bet. What song did Kevin sing?

334. How do you spell candy with only two letters?

335. I run swiftly but never take steps, I fall down but never rest. What am I?

336. What is offered by many, taken by few, yet can be invaluable? It's a six-letter word.

337. I connect two people, yet I only physically touch one. What am I?

338. I start in little but I end in full, you'll find me in half and complete. What am I?

339. Never ahead, ever behind,

    Yet flying swiftly past;

    For a child, I last forever,

    For adults, I'm gone too fast.

    What am I?

340. I have no wings, but I will fly. Leaves are my favourite food. What am I?

341. Lighter than what I'm made of, more of me is hidden than is seen. What am I?

342. What does this picture say?

343. I'm vital for your everyday life, but staring at me is not so wise. What am I?

344. I come in many types, but the one you can pick won't fulfil its role. What am I?

345. I'm one of many, yet easily missed. your stability relies on my subtle assist. I'm the foundation, the solid base. Without me, you'd stumble in any chase. What am I?

346. A red house is made out of red bricks. A white house is made out of white bricks. What is a green house made out of?

347. What does this picture say?

348. I am the beginning of the end and the end of the start. What am I?

349. In a race, Caleb ranked 50th from both the top and bottom. What is the total number of runners who participated in the race?

350. Call me gold, I am good.

   Call me stone, I am empty.

   Call me glass, I am fragile.

   Call me cold, I am cruel.

   What am I??

351. In the middle of the night, a man was discovered outside a store, unconscious and bleeding from his head. A brick lay next to him. When the police arrived, they decided to arrest him. Why?

352. Seven brothers, five work all day. The other two, just play or pray. What are they?

353. What are the next two letters in this sequence: M, T, W, T, F...?

FIX ME PLEASE!

354. How do you fix a cracked pumpkin?

355. A builder has 12 screws, all of which look identical and should weigh the same. However, one of the screws is defective and weighs less than the others. The builder only has a balance scale to work with. He can place the screws on each side of the scale to see if they weigh the same. How can he find the defective screw in the fewest number of weighings?

356. I was born twice in my life. Once from an egg, and once wrapped in silk. What am I?

357. I am a big box that runs up and down. What am I?

358. Flat as a leaf, round as a ring, has two eyes, can't see a thing. What am I?

359. What is a delicious treat that has no beginning, end, or middle?

360. A group of friends participated in a race. Friend A finished three minutes before friend B. Friend C crossed the finish line five minutes before friend D. Friend D took four more minutes than friend A. In what order do they cross the finish line?

361. If you multiply all the numbers on a calculator together, what number do you get?

362. What does this picture say?

HAHANDND

363. Use me well and I am everybody. Scratch my back and I am nobody. What am I?

364. What is it that, given one, you'll have either two or none?

365. A time when they're green, a time when they're brown,

     But both of these times, cause me to frown.

     But just in between, for a very short while,

     They're perfect and yellow, and cause me to smile!

     What are they?

# BONUS RIDDLES

366. Luke and his wife lived in the countryside. One day, Luke's wife became sick, and he called the local doctor for help. When the doctor answered the call, Luke expressed his concern, saying, "Doctor, I think my wife may have appendicitis."

The doctor responded, "That's not possible! I removed her appendix three years ago."

However, when Luke's wife underwent a medical examination, it was indeed confirmed that she had appendicitis.

How could this be possible?

367. There's a ship in the water, and it has a 5-foot ladder attached to its side. If the tide is rising at the rate of one foot an hour, how long will it take for the water to cover the ladder?

368. Once upon a time, there was a clever innkeeper with many friends. One night, they all gambled at his inn. When the candles went out, someone stole the money!

The innkeeper was upset, but he had an idea. He put his rooster in a big old kettle from the fireplace and told everyone to touch it in the dark. He told them the rooster would crow if the thief touched it.

When they touched the kettle, the rooster stayed quiet. However, as soon as the candles were lit again, the innkeeper knew who had stolen the money.

How did he know?

369. A man is locked in a cell with a dirt floor and a window that's too high to reach. There's no food or water, and the only thing in the cell is a shovel. The man knows he has to escape, or he'll die of dehydration. It will take too long for him to dig a tunnel out of the cell. What should he do?

370. A man enters a store and secretly takes a $100 bill from the cash register without the store owner knowing. He then buys items worth $70 using the stolen $100 bill and receives $30 in change from the owner. How much money did the owner lose in total?

371. What are the next two letters in this sequence? J, F, M, A, M, J, J, A, S, O....

372. What are the next two letters in this sequence? W, A, T, N, T, L, I....

373. A wealthy Indian man sent his son to the market with one coin. The man told his son to buy something to feed the cows, something to plant in the garden, something for them to eat, and something for them to drink. The son could only buy one item. What did he buy?

374. A truck driver and a doctor are both in love with a woman named Chloe. The truck driver had to go on a week-long journey, and before departing, he gave Chloe seven apples. Why?

375. Akbar, the third Mughal Emperor of India, was a wise ruler. He was also a very curious man, and he loved to learn new things. One day, Akbar was talking to his advisor, Birbal, when he asked, "Birbal, can you write a sentence for me that will make me feel sad when I am happy, and happy when I am sad?"

Birbal thought for a moment, and then he wrote down something that fit the requirements.

Can you guess what did he write?

# ANSWERS

1. Silence.

2. Lunch and Dinner.

3. A t-shirt.

4. A die (as in single dice).

5. 9 in the family – Mr (1), Mrs (2), 6 daughters (3-8), 1 brother (9) – all 6 daughters share the same brother.

6. A blackboard.

7. Lucy.

8. A one (or two) pence piece.

9. There were only 3 people on the fishing trip: a grandfather, his son, and the son's son. So, there were two fathers and two sons, but only three people total!

10. Queue  - Q.

11. A picture is worth a thousand words.

# ANSWERS 12-26

12. 10 o'clock plus 3 hours is 1 o'clock, so 8 o'clock plus 6 hours is 2 o'clock.

13. Drop the first letter – Seven becomes even!

14. He got it put in a box which was 210cm long and 30cm high, then the rod could fit into the diagonal of the box and be posted to him within the rules of the postal service.

15. Yesterday, today, and tomorrow.

16. Footsteps.

17. An umbrella.

18. A sponge.

19. A hole.

20. The man wrote "your exact weight" on the paper.

21. 12 – all months have at least 28 days.

22. A Secret.

23. A bed – it has a head and 4 legs but there is just 1 foot of a bed.

24. Jon finished in 2nd place – he overtook 2nd place to become the 2nd in the race.

25. Your name.

26. The first shop (the messy shop) because that barber must have given the barber from the 2nd shop a neat haircut.

27. Fire.

28. The letter "I".

29. A towel.

30. Time flies.

31. A bar of soap.

32. Its lid.

33. Cutting corners.

34. When Abi was 8 her sister would have been 4. Now 2 years later Abi is 10, and therefore her sister is also 2 years older, so she's 6.

35. 1,2,3 because $(1+2+3) = (1 \times 2 \times 3) = 6$.

36. They both weigh the same – a kilogram.

37. A stamp.

38. A computer keyboard (the Enter key is sometimes known as the Return key).

39. Your left elbow.

40. The letter "R".

41. A carrot.

42. Short.

43. An egg.

44. A candle.

45. Light  (or sound).

46. The dictionary.

47. Yes – buildings can't jump!

48. A friend in need is a friend indeed.

49. February as it has just 28 days and nights (or 29 on a leap year).

50. Memories.

51. On Steve's head.

52. Take away the 2 letters F and E from FIVE to get IV which is the Roman numeral for 4.

53. Top secret.

54. There are three ducks in total. Imagine a line of three ducks: D1-D2-D3. D1 and D2 are in front of D3; D2 and D3 are behind D1; and D2 is the one duck in the middle.

55. 4 minutes – each cat catches 1 mouse in 4 mins.

56. Only once, after that, you'll be subtracting 6 from 30.

57. 32 – if you think of each spoke and space as 1 pair, then it's easier to understand that the last spoke and space come back to meet the first one.

58. On a map.

59. A see-saw.

60. Heroine – he, her, hero, heroine.

61. It would be cheaper to take 2 friends at the same time (total of 3 tickets), as if he went twice with 1 friend he'd be paying for himself twice (total of 4 tickets).

62. First Aid.

63. Envelope.

64. A peacock.

65. A kiwi (there is a kiwi fruit, there is also the flightless kiwi bird that lives in New Zealand, and a slang term for someone from New Zealand is a kiwi).

66. They were on opposite sides of the river to start with, so the first fox crossed in the boat and handed it over to the 2nd fox to make the journey across, but in the other direction.

67. You are under arrest.

68. A lie.

69. A promise.

70. £400. You bought a racing bike for £800 and sold it for £1000, making a profit of £1000 - £800 = £200. Later, you bought it back for £1100 and sold it again for £1300, making another profit of £1300 - £1100 = £200. In total, you made £400.

71. Monkey and donkey.

72. A window.

73. Spider.

74. Rudolf, the red nose reindeer (Red Nose Rain Deer).

75. A staircase.

76. A table.

77. A cold.

78. A fence.

79. Your nose.

80. 9 (4+5).

81. 31st of December – today is 1st Jan so the day before yesterday was the day before this person's birthday (they were 11). Then on their birthday (31 Dec), they turned 12. Today they are 12 and later this year they'll turn 13, so next year they'll be 14.

82. There are 4 sisters, and 3 brothers – because Alice had 3 sisters and 3 brothers. Each brother has 2 other brothers and a total of 4 sisters.

83. The word "ton".

84. Stone. If you remove the "st" from the word "stone", you are left with the word "one".

85. Coffin.

86. Nothing.

87. Water.

88. Baby elephants.

89. Sweet dreams.

90. The letter "E".

91. A chick in an egg.

92. Charcoal.

93. A road.

94. Bookkeeper.

95. A leaf.

96. A sword.

97. $99 + 9/9 = 99+1 = 100$.

98. The letter "R".

99. Your dad.

100. Too funny for words (2 Funny 4 Words).

101. You'd have 2 apples.

102. No dirt in a hole.

103. The dictionary.

104. The word "incorrectly".

105. John weighs meat because he works at a butcher's.

106. SWIMS.

107. The post office.

108. Age.

109. Your word.

110. It's impossible to break a concrete floor with an egg.

111. A teapot.

112. Giraffe.

113. Smiles, because there is a mile between each "s".

114. A feather.

115. An onion.

116. The wind.

117. A question you can never truthfully answer "yes" to is "Are you lying right now?"

    If you are lying right now, you are not telling the truth, so you cannot answer yes to this question. This is a paradox because it is impossible to be both lying and not lying at the same time.

118. Be on time (Bee on time).

119. A plant.

120. The man in the picture is Harry's son.

121. A palm.

122. To make the number one disappear, add a "G" in front of it and it becomes "gone".

123. Fishing for compliments (Fish in 4 compliments).

124. Echo.

125. A joke.

126. The future.

127. Edam (Edam is a Dutch cheese, and the word "Edam" is "made" spelt backwards.)

128. A leg.

129. Darkness.

130. Ears.

131. Traffic light.

132. Roosters don't lay eggs.

133. A clock.

134. A mirror.

135. The ruler costs $1.

136. Eight eggs left unbroken.

137. No, it won't be sunny because in 48 hours it will be the middle of the night again.

138. An anchor.

139. 2 feet. Dogs have paws, while pigs, cows, and sheep have hooves, only the farmer has feet.

140. Once upon a time (1s upon a time).

141. Leaves.

142. An icicle.

143. Light.

144. Your brain.

145. An eyeball.

146. Breakfast.

147. A gummy bear.

148. A glove.

149. Friday.

    This riddle can be solved by using deductive reasoning.

    First, we know that tomorrow is not Wednesday or Thursday, so today cannot be Tuesday or Wednesday.

    Second, we know that yesterday was not Friday or Saturday, so today cannot be Saturday or Sunday.

    That leaves us with the possibilities of Monday, Thursday, and Friday. However, we also know that today is not Thursday or Monday. Therefore, the only remaining possibility is Friday. So, today is Friday.

150. A watermelon. The green house is the outer rind, the white house is the inside of the rind, the red house is the flesh, and the babies are the individual seeds within the red flesh.

151. Halfway; it'd be running out of the woods once it has reached the halfway point.

152. A piano.

153. The letter "R".

154. Andy has no brothers. The three doctors are his sisters.

155. Rain.

156. The letter "D".

157. Racecar.

158. The 7th.

159. Because Mary and Lisa are two of a set of triplets.

160. Coffee. Based on the pattern provided, Tilly would be drinking coffee, as her name contains a double "L" like the other coffee drinkers in the pattern.

161. A deck of cards.

162. Missing you (Missing U).

163. A door.

164. Jack should light the match first. With the match lit, he could then proceed to light the candle, wood stove, or lamp as needed.

165. Becky. The order of their ages from youngest to oldest: Ben - Pete - Becky - Annie - Dan. The middle child would be Becky.

166. A reflection.

167. Lily's one-storey house doesn't have any stairs since it has only one level.

168. She fell off from the bottom rung.

169. Robin Hood (ROB in HOOD)

170. He was walking, not driving.

171. A volcano.

172. To help the farmer and his animal friends cross the river safely, they can follow these steps:

    a. First, the farmer takes the hen across the river in the boat and leaves her on the other side.

    b. Then, the farmer comes back to the starting side (where the corn and the fox are) with an empty boat.

    c. Now, the farmer takes the fox across the river in the boat to the other side.

    d. After bringing the fox to the other side, the farmer leaves the fox there but takes the hen back to the starting side in the boat.

    e. Once the farmer reaches the starting side, he leaves the hen there and takes the corn with him in the boat to the other side.

    f. After safely bringing the corn to the other side, the farmer leaves the corn there and goes back alone to the starting side.

    g. Now, the farmer takes the hen one more time and brings her across the river.

    By following these steps, the farmer successfully gets all three things—the corn, the hen, and the fox—across the river without any harm coming to them.

173. Because he was born on February 29. Since February 29 occurs only once every four years, despite living for 100 chronological years, the old man would have only celebrated his 25th birthday just before his death.

# ANSWERS 174-177

174. The river was frozen.

175. The letter "M".

176. The number seven is the only number that contains two syllables.

177. 21 handshakes.

Let's imagine there are seven people named A, B, C, D, E, F, and G. Each of them shakes hands with everyone else once.

Person A shakes hands with B, C, D, E, F, and G. That's 6 handshakes.

Person B shakes hands with C, D, E, F, and G. That's 5 handshakes.

Person C shakes hands with D, E, F, and G. That's 4 handshakes.

Person D shakes hands with E, F, and G. That's 3 handshakes.

Person E shakes hands with F and G. That's 2 handshakes.

Person F shakes hands with G. That's 1 handshake.

Now, if we add up all the handshakes, we get:

6 + 5 + 4 + 3 + 2 + 1 = 21.

So, in this group of seven people, there are 21 handshakes in total.

178. The third room. The power is cut off in the house, so the exposed electrical wires would not pose a danger.

179. Underdogs.

180. A nose.

181. On the corner.

182. A dewdrop. A dewdrop is small, resembling fragile glass, and can be seen as a tiny bead when it forms on grass due to condensation.

183. Bob and Sarah are on a tandem and Alice is on a unicycle.

184. Anna.

185. The letter "G".

186. Memories.

187. Read between the lines.

188. It was daytime.

189. An oval.

190. A leek (leak).

191. Mushroom.

192. A book.

193. Jerry ordered two pizzas, one Margherita and one Hawaiian.

194. A blueberry.

195. 10 animals were making their way to the river (1 rabbit, 3 monkeys, and 6 parrots). However, it is unclear from the given information whether or not the elephants were heading towards the river.

196. The pocket has one thing - a hole.

197. The number 8. When the digit 8 is turned on its side, it resembles the symbol for infinity (∞), which signifies being without bounds or limitless. However, if you cut the number 8 in half horizontally, it splits into two separate parts, resulting in two zeros (0), which symbolise nothing.

198. I have so many problems.

199. Neither of them is closer because when they meet, they're both at the same spot, therefore they are both the same distance from London.

200. Facebook.

201. The stars.

202. Corn on the cob.

203. Few.

204. The living room.

205. Just one. As soon as you put an orange in an empty fruit bowl, it's not empty anymore.

206. Broken heart.

207. An earthworm.

208. His car has four regular wheels, one steering wheel, and a spare wheel (4+1+1 = 6).

209. Your eyes.

210. Water.

211. Toothpaste.

212. She throws the ball into the air, and it falls back down due to the force of gravity.

213. Money.

214. The number 1.

    Every number 1-9 appears 10 times as the units digit (1, 11, 21, 31...).

    Every number 1-9 appears 10 times as the tens digit (10, 11, 12, 13...).

    However, only the number 1 has an extra occurrence as the hundreds digit (100).

    So the number 1 appears most frequently.

215. NOON.

216. Dozens.

217. A hole.

218. Sand. Sand can be used to build up castles, as it is a common material for constructing sandcastles and other structures. Over time, sand can erode and break down mountains and rocks through processes like wind and water erosion. Sand can get into people's eyes and make

them temporarily blind. Sand can also be used to make glass, which is used in lenses to help people see.

219.  Paradise (pair of dice).

220.  Emma ordered the pizza on New Year's Eve and it arrived in the new year.

221.  The bear is white. The only place where all sides of a house would face south is at the North Pole, and the only bears that live at the North Pole are polar bears.

222.  There are twenty 9s. (9, 19, 29, 39, 49, 59, 69, 79, 89, 90, 91, 92, 93, 94, 95, 96, 97, 98, 99).

223.  Place a decimal point to make 3.4.

224.  A sad zebra.

225.  Three blind mice. All the "I"s (eyes) are missing.

226.  John is 12 years old.

Let's assume John's current age is x.

According to the given information, "In two years, I will be twice as old as I was five years ago." This can be written as:

$x + 2 = 2(x - 5)$

Now, let's solve the equation:

$x + 2 = 2x - 10$

Bringing the variables to one side and the constants to the other side:

2x - x = 2 + 10

x = 12

Therefore, John is currently 12 years old.

227. Alphabet.

228. It's 9pm.

The time that is "as long after one o'clock in the afternoon as it was before one o'clock in the morning" is halfway across the clock face from 1, which is 7.

We can determine it was 7pm because it was after 1pm and before 1am. If 7pm was two hours ago, then the current time is 9pm.

229. Your breath.

230. A jigsaw puzzle.

231. A rainbow.

232. A needle.

233. A potato.

234. A gift.

235. Pun.

236. The lion got $20. They were paid according to the number of legs and for each leg they have they got $5.

237. Blue (Blew).

238. A pillow.

239. Hole-in-one. In golf, a hole-in-one is an occasion when someone's ball goes into the hole the first time they hit it.

240. Plates and cutlery.

241. Friendship.

242. The number 9.

243. It will take 16 days. The snail progresses by 1 metre daily, which means that after 15 days, it will have reached a height of 15 metres. On the 16th day, the snail will finally make it to the top without sliding back, successfully escaping the hole.

244. Design (D sign).

245. Zero.

246. A scarecrow.

247. An eye.

248. The bus driver is you.

249. The human being. A human crawls on all fours as a baby ("four legs in the morning"), walks on two legs as an adult ("two legs in the afternoon"), and uses a cane or walking stick in old age ("three legs in the evening"). When a human dies, they are no longer able to walk, so they have "no legs at night.

250. The question is "What time is it?".

251. C (sea).

252. They are all married, so no single person on board.

253. Day and night.

254. A white carnation (car nation).

255. It's today, Monday.

256. Time.

257. Shadow.

258. The third man in the boat was bald and didn't have any hair to get wet.

259. You're standing back to back.

260. The rock makes a splash and gets wet.

261. Clouds.

262. The 8-letter word that fits the given criteria is "starting." When consecutive letters are removed, it becomes "sting," "sing," "sin," "in," and finally "I," which is a valid word.

263. Good looking.

264. 23. The age difference between you and your dad is 23 years (31 - 8 = 23). Since your dad's age is currently twice as old as yours and the age difference remains the same, your current age would be 23 years old.

265. Hands.

266. Ten tickles (tentacles).

267. There's no such thing as half a hole.

268.  A is D's grandfather.

269.  A pea.

270.  Missing LINK.

271.  She is playing chess with Carol.

272.  A dress (address).

273.  A doorbell.

274.  Mount Everest. Even before it was officially discovered and measured, it was still the highest mountain in the world.

275.  2 minutes. It will take 1 minute for the front of the train to travel through the tunnel. It will take 1 more minute for the back of the train to clear the tunnel. So, it will take 2 minutes for the entire train to travel through the tunnel.

276.  Art. When the letter K is added, it transforms into "kart".

277.  Shoes.

278.  You can find them both in the middle of water.

279.  Syllables.

280.  The person is a child and too short to reach the button for the 15th floor in the elevator. On rainy days, he uses an umbrella to press the button.

281.  Two. The inside and the outside.

282.  Jack in the Box.

283.  19 cookies.

Alice has 4 cookies now.

Before sharing half with her brother, she had 8 cookies.

Before she ate one herself, she had 9 cookies.

Before sharing half with her sister, she had 18 cookies.

Before she ate one herself, she had 19 cookies.

So at the very beginning, Alice had 19 cookies.

284. Ian.

285. None of them. Because bananas don't grow on coconut trees.

286. Wholesome.

287. A shoe!

288. Y (Why).

289. Ice.

290. He was blind and using braille.

291. Cool music.

292. He could reach his food because the rope wasn't tied to anything else.

293. A comb.

294. A wave.

295. You need to pick 5 socks to guarantee a matching pair. The worst-case scenario is that you pick 4 socks of different colours before you pick a 5th sock. Once you

pick the 5th sock, it is certain to match one of the previously selected socks, so you'll have a matching pair.

296.    Up to you (Up two U).

297.    Let's begin by picking a fruit from the box that says "Apples and Oranges." If you find an apple in that box, it means the box is filled with apples. So, we change the label on that box to "Apples."

Now, remember that all the boxes initially had the wrong labels. The box that originally said "Oranges" cannot contain oranges, and since we have already found the box with only apples it can only be the box containing both apples and oranges. We change its label to "Apples and Oranges."

Lastly, the box that used to say "Apples" can only contain oranges since we have already found the boxes with only apples and both apples and oranges. So, it should be labelled as "Oranges."

By following these steps, all the boxes will have the correct labels!

298.    It wasn't raining.

299.    A shadow.

300.    The cowboy's horse is named Friday.

301.    The letter "T".

302.    The letter "S".

303.    Handsome (Hand Sum).

304. A keyhole.

305. Gloves.

306. The letter "V".

307. The gift is sent through the mail multiple times. Here's how they do it:

   a. Paul puts the surprise gift in a box and locks it with his lock. He keeps the key for himself.

   b. Paul sends the locked box to Jane.

   c. When Jane gets the box, she adds her own lock to it. She keeps the key for herself.

   d. Jane sends the box back to Paul with two locks on it.

   e. When Paul receives the box with both locks on it, he uses his key to open his lock and remove it.

   f. Paul sends the box back to Jane with one lock on it.

   g. When Jane receives the box, she can unlock her lock with her key and open the box.

   By using dual locks, Paul and Jane make sure the gift stays locked during shipping, but Jane can still open it in the end.

308. 9 years. The tree doubled in height each year, so it reached half its maximum height in the year before it reached its maximum height. Therefore, it took the tree 9 years to reach half its maximum height.

# ANSWERS 309-319

309.  A chicken.

310.  Dimensions. A square has width and length, a line has just length, and a point has no dimensions.

311.  Syllables.

312.  The abbreviations can be interpreted as follows:

    a.  60 S in a M - 60 seconds in a minute.

    b.  28 D in F - 28 days in February.

    c.  12 M in a Y - 12 months in a year.

    d.  4 S in a Y - 4 seasons in a year.

    e.  5 F on a H - 5 fingers on a hand.

    f.  2 E on Y F - 2 eyes on your face.

    g.  7 H P B - 7 Harry Potter Books.

    h.  8 P of the M - 8 phases of the Moon.

313.  A chair, a bed, and a toothbrush.

314.  Jon slept at night.

315.  The strawberry.

316.  The police knew the woman committed the crime because she drove straight to the crime scene without being told where it was.

317.  The letter "W".

318.  Three wise men (three Ys men).

319.  A pencil.

# ANSWERS 320-334

320. There are 1461 days. Normally, a year has 365 days. But every four years, we have a special year called a leap year, which has one extra day. Therefore, in total, there would be 365 x 3 + 366 = 1461 days in four years.

321. They were born in different time zones.

322. A snowman.

323. News

324. A vacuum cleaner.

325. I love you (Eye Love U).

326. Because they just finished a March.

327. A bat.

328. A frog.

329. A garbage truck.

330. A balloon.

331. 2 kilograms. The question says that the brick weighs 1 kilogram plus half of its weight. This means that half of the brick's weight is 1 kilogram. So, the total weight 1+1=2 kilograms.

332. 3 inches. If Abbie made 3 cuts, she divided the rope into 4 equal sections. Each section would be 12/4 = 3 inches long.

333. He sang the Happy Birthday song.

334. C and Y.

335. Waterfall.

336. Advice.

337. A wedding ring.

338. The letter "L".

339. Childhood.

340. A caterpillar.

341. An iceberg.

342. I understand (eye under stand).

343. The Sun.

344. A lock.

345. A toe.

346. Glass.

347. Corner shop.

348. The letter "T".

349. 99 runners. There are 49 runners ahead of Caleb and 49 runners behind him, making a total of 99 participants.

350. A heart.

351. The man got hurt while trying to rob a store. He threw a brick at the shop window that bounced back and hit him.

352. The days of the week. Monday, Tuesday, Wednesday, Thursday, and Friday are the five working days. Saturday

and Sunday are the two days of rest when people can play or pray.

353. The next two letters in the sequence are "S" and "S" representing the days of the week: Saturday and Sunday.

354. With a pumpkin patch.

355. The builder can find the defective screw in 3 weighings. Here is the strategy:

   a. Divide the screws into three groups of four.

   b. Weigh the first two groups against each other.

   c. If the two groups weigh the same, the defective screw is in the third group. Otherwise, the defective screw is in the lighter group.

   d. Divide the group that contains the defective screw into two groups of two.

   e. Weigh the two groups against each other. The defective screw is in the lighter group.

   f. Weigh the two screws in the lighter group. The lighter screw is the defective one.

356. A silkworm. The first time is when it hatches from an egg. The second time is when it emerges from the cocoon as an adult moth.

357. An elevator.

358. A button. Buttons are flat and round, and they have two holes in them that look like eyes.

359.  A doughnut.

360.  The order of finishing was C - A - B - D.

361.  0. The number zero (0) is included on the calculator number pad, and any number multiplied by zero results in zero.

362.  Hand in hand.

363.  Mirror.

364.  A choice. If you are given one choice, you can either choose it or not choose it. If you choose it, you will have two choices: the one you chose and the one you didn't choose. If you don't choose it, you will have no choice.

365.  Bananas

366.  Luke had married another woman after his first wife had her appendix removed by the doctor. So when Luke's second wife fell ill with appendicitis, it was a different person who needed the surgery.

367.  The water will never cover the ladder, since the ship will rise with the tide.

368.  The innkeeper was clever. He knew that the thief would be afraid of the rooster crowing, so he asked everyone to touch the kettle in the dark. The thief didn't touch the kettle because he didn't want to risk the rooster crowing and giving him away.

The kettle was covered in soot, because it was from a fireplace, so everyone else who touched it got soot on their hands. The thief, however, didn't touch the kettle, so he was the only one with clean hands. This is how the innkeeper knew who the thief was.

369. He used a shovel to dig and make a big pile of dirt right under the window. After two days of digging, he climbed up the dirt pile and escaped through the window.

370. $100. The store owner lost $30 in change given to the man and $70 worth of items purchased with the stolen money. Therefore, the owner lost a total of $100.

371. The letters in the sequence are the first letters of the months of the year, so the next two letters are N (November) and D (December).

372. The letters are the first letters of the words in the question, "What are the next two letters in this sequence?", so the next two letters in the sequence are T (this) and S (sequence).

373. A watermelon. The flesh can be eaten, the juice can be drunk, the rind can be used to feed the cows, and the seeds can be planted in the garden.

374. Because "An apple a day keeps the doctor away."

375. He wrote, "This too shall pass." It means that everything in life is temporary. Both good and bad times will pass.

# ALSO AVAILABLE IN AMAZON:

**ISBN** 979-8561671821

**ISBN** 979-8754213760

**ISBN** 979-8363199271

**ISBN** 979-8837831515

**ISBN** 979-8771423029

**ISBN** 979-8575928928

**ISBN** 979-8569221776